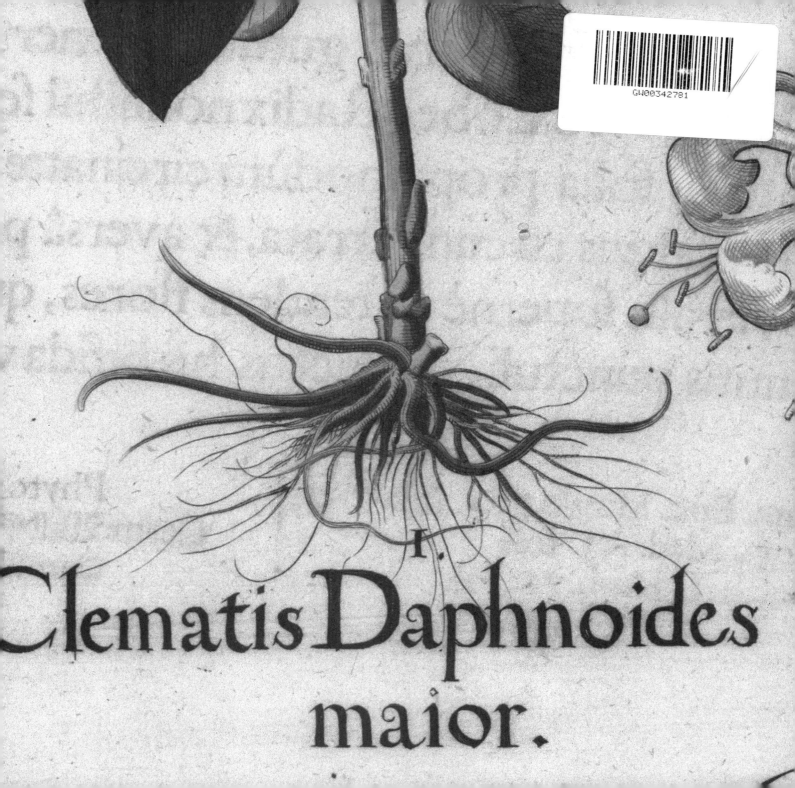

Clematis Daphnoides

maior.

IN THE

Garden

IN THE

Garden

Blooming Stories

Edited by JOHN AND KIRSTEN MILLER

STACKPOLE BOOKS

LIBRARY OF CONGRESS CATALOGUING IN PUBLICATION DATA
In the garden: blooming stories / edited by John and Kirsten Miller.
p.   cm.   ISBN 0-8117-0906-X
1. Gardens—Literary collections. I. Miller, John, 1959- .
II. Miller, Kirsten 1963- .
PN6071.G27I5 1994 808.8'036—dc20
93—34672 CIP

Printed in Hong Kong.
Page 132 constitutes a continuation of the copyright page.

Editing, design, and composition: Big Fish Books

Stackpole Books
5067 Ritter Road
Mechanicsburg, PA 17055.

Plates courtesy of the W. Graham Arader III Gallery.

Flora dispensing Her Favours on the Earth

London, Published by Dr Thornton, May 1, 1807

DR. ROBERT JOHN THORNTON
{The Temple of Flora}

CONTENTS

II.
Halicacabum vulgatius.

I.
Pisum cordatum

III.
Halicacabum seu Sola
num Indicum Camerarij.

I.
Stramonia.

III.
Botris Dracontiæmaior.

II.
Halimi.

BASIL BESLER

{Hortus Eystettensis}

John and Kirsten Miller

INTRODUCTION

 T WAS WILL and Ariel Durant who suggested that gardening was the most ephemeral of all the arts. Certainly, what a gardener plants in the cool of the evening will not be what he sees the next sunup. A perfectly open rose is not the next hour. To catch an instant—a perfect instant—in a garden's constant change has been a challenge to many an artist.

Four of the most impressive attempts illustrate our book. Two of our brushmen were not artists per se, but pharmacists. Historically, pharmacists held lofty positions in society: analyzing patient's complaints, dispensing appropriate reliefs, and often, dabbling in painting.

BY DAY, BASIL Besler was a quiet Nuremberg apothecary. It was his moonlighting—as the boss of the Prince of Bavaria's garden—where he truly

flourished. Under Besler's care, roses climbed skyward, melons grew bulky.
So pleased was the Prince, he promised full patronage for Besler's deepest dream:
a pictorial volume of all garden species. But this was no simple task: the printing
press was yet to be invented, so books in the early 1600s were basically text,
with art restricted to the cover (or, if the publisher was in a particularly
swashbuckling mood, a frontispiece).

But sixteen years after it was started, Besler's massive *Hortus Eystettensis*
was completed. When we say massive... not only did the volume contain 374
full- color plates representing 1,000 plants and flowers, but each painting measured a dizzying two feet tall!

Besler was praised in particular for his depiction of roots, heretofore
snubbed as dirty underparts. The lovely winding roots and extraordinary
calligraphy ensured a spot in history for *Hortus Eystettensis*.

A HUNDRED YEARS later, another pharmacist with equal brush flair produced the behemoth *Phytanthoza Iconographia*, a reeling four-volume set containing over 1,200 hand-colored plates of fruits, flowers, and vegetables. The man
behind it all was the German-born Johann Weinmann, who relied on his pharma-
ceutical skills to give this book a unique twist: the organization of plants according to their curative powers. As a pharmacist, Weinmann had a keen interest in
these matters. In fact, in the 1800s many a wealthy landowner had his own personal apothecary charged with tending a garden purely dedicated to studying
species and their restorative possibilities.

Another unusual feature of *Phytanthoza* was its groundbreaking use of
mezzotint. Engravings in 1745 were basically coloring books: simple black line

drawings with patches of color filled in. If you look closely, you'll see Weinmann took this a step further, shading and coloring the lines of the base drawing, giving the overall engraving a lush, visceral feel.

ACROSS THE CHANNEL in England, George Brookshaw was not to be outdone by the Germans. The artist stripped his flowers and fruits from their natural foliage and, in a decidedly modern—almost architectural—way, arranged them on stark white and brown painted backgrounds. Brookshaw had discovered a method known as aquatint printing, which yielded blindingly vivid colors and a grand sweep of tonal variations. He took full advantage of this process; the effect was startling.

Certainly Britishers were startled when *A Collection of the Most Esteemed Fruits* hit the streets in 1812. But despite Brookshaw's unorthodox approach, it was hard not to be won over by these pleasing paintings. Even critics grumpily admitted the book was "one of the finest colour plate books in existence."

PERHAPS THE MOST eccentric of our artists is Dr. Robert John Thornton. As a boy, Thornton snubbed routine playground games, concentrating instead on the assemblage of a backyard aviary containing every species of English hawk (most collected by himself). A foreshadowing for a particularly singular career...

It was upon inheriting his family's fortune that Thornton quit his physician's job and announced his intention to leave his mark on the world by creating a volume surpassing in "scope, illustration, paper and typography, any publication produced in any European country." It would be *The Temple of Flora,* a collection of botanical drawings, and would be a tribute to England—and himself.

The brilliance of the *The Temple* would be Thornton's imaginative drawings. Rather than workaday plant portraits, the book would feature flora basking in fanciful settings of the doctor's own creation. In 1807, after eight years of work, Thornton purchased an art gallery and unveiled his masterpiece.

The public was appalled. People in 1807 London liked their botanical drawings accurate, not embellished or in ridiculous surroundings. And no one was particularly amused to discover that Thornton painted only one of the pictures (the rest he "directed"). Yes, *The Temple* was a flop; the original optimistic print run was scaled down to a pitiful 30 copies. To top it off, a subsequent lottery of the bits and pieces was roundly snubbed. The sullen doctor returned to his medicine.

GARDEN MEDITATION IS not the exclusive turf of the painter, of course. In our pages, we see writers equally mesmerized by fruits of the earth: read the melancholy Raymond Carver, the brooding Sylvia Plath, the worshipful Pablo Neruda, and Homer in veritable marching spirit. There's Frances Hodgson Burnett's magical garden and the awe-inspiring Hanging Gardens of Babylon. There's Vincent van Gogh painting his garden; Helen Keller feeling hers.

Besler, Dr. Thornton, Raymond Carver, Helen Keller: Different gardeners in different gardens, but after the same thing...a fleeting glimpse, a moment of meditation on a special plot of ground, from whence we all come, where we toil, where we reap food for the belly, rest for the eye.

> *This is the garden: colours come and go,*
> *frail azures fluttering from night's outer wing*
> —*e.e. cummings*

—J M , K M

GARDENS AND FIRELIGHT

O LEFT AND RIGHT, outside, he saw an orchard

closed by a pale—four spacious acres planted

with trees in bloom or weighted down for picking:

pear trees, pomegranates, brilliant apples,

luscious figs, and olives ripe and dark.

Fruit never failed upon these trees: winter

and summer time they bore for through the year

the breathing Westwind ripened all in turn—

so one pear came to prime, and then another

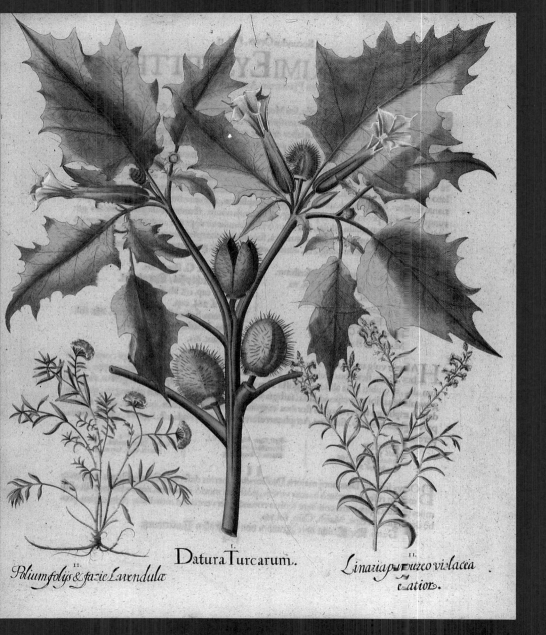

Datura Turcarum.

Polium folijs & facie Lavendulæ

Linaziap puzeo vi lacea e atior.

and so with apples, figs and the vine's fruit

empurpled in the royal vineyard there.

Currants were dried at one end, on a platform

bare to the sun, beyond the vintage arbors

and vats the vintners trod; while near at hand

were new grapes barely formed as the green bloom fell,

or half-ripe clusters, faintly coloring.

After the vines came rows of vegetables

of all kinds that flourish in every season,

and through the garden plots and orchard ran

channels from one clear fountain, while another

gushed through a pipe under the courtyard entrance

to serve the house and all who came for water.

These were the gifts of heaven to Alkínoös.

Colette

The Ways of Wistaria

 HOPE THAT IT is still alive, and that it will go on living for a long time, that flourishing, irrepressible despot, a centenarian at least twice over: the wistaria that spills over the garden walls of the house where I was born, and down into the rue des Vignes. Proof of its vitality was brought to me last year by a spry and charming lady pillager ... A black dress, a head of white hair, a sexagenarian agility—all this had jumped, in the rue des Vignes, deserted as in bygone days, until it had grabbed hold of and made off with one of the wistaria's long terminal withes, which ended up flowering in Paris, on the divan bed

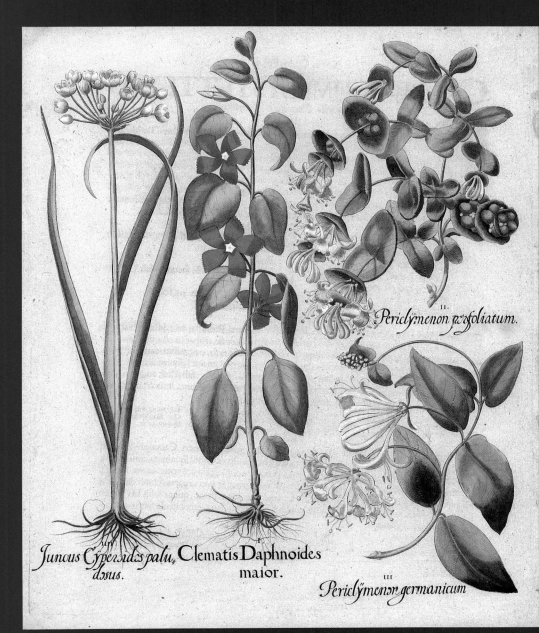

Periclymenon perfoliatum.

Juncus Cyperoides palu-
dosus.

Clematis Daphnoides
maior.

Periclymenon germanicum

where I am bound by my arthritis. Besides its fragrance, the butterfly-shaped flower retained a small hymenoptera, an inchworm, and a ladybug, all direct and unexpected from Saint-Sauveur, in Puisaye.

To tell the truth about this wistaria, in which I discovered, here on my bed table, a fragrance, a blue-violet color, and a bearing all vaguely recognizable, I remember that it had a bad reputation all along that narrow domain bounded by a wall and defended by an iron railing. It dates from long ago, from before my mother Sido's first marriage. Its mad profusion in May and its meager resurgence in August and September perfume my earliest childhood memories. It was as heavy with bees as with blossoms and would hum like a cymbal whose sound spreads without ever fading away, more beautiful each year, until the time when Sido, leaning over its flowery burden out of curiosity, let out the little "Ah-hah!" of great discoveries long anticipated: the wistaria had begun to pull up the iron railing.

As there could be no question, in Sido's domain, of killing a wistaria, it exercised, and exercises still, its decided strength. I saw it lift an impressive length of railing up out of the stone and mortar, brandish it in the air, bend the bars in plantlike imitation of its own twists and turns, and show a marked preference for an ophidian intertwining of bar and trunk, eventually embedding the one in the other. In time it met up with its neighbor the honeysuckle, the sweet, charming, red-flowered honeysuckle. At first it seemed not to notice, and then slowly smothered it as a snake suffocates a bird.

As I watched, I learned that its overwhelming beauty served a murderous strength. I learned how it covers, strangles, adorns, ruins, and shores up. The Ampelopsis is a mere boy compared with the coils, woody even when new, of the wistaria …

I visited the Désert de Retz one beautiful, torrid day when everything conspired toward a siesta and disturbing dreams. I will never go back there, for fear of finding that that place, made for tempered nightmares, has paled. Muddy, rush-filled water slept there at the foot of a kiosk furnished with broken-down writing tables, footless stools, and other unexplained pieces of furniture floating around. I cling to the memory of a truncated tower, topped off abruptly by a beveled roof. Inside, it was divided into little cells around a spiral staircase, each of which assumed, roughly, the shape of a trapezoid …

O world, how full you are of mysteries and inconveniences for one by no means a born geometrician, struggling in vain to describe the

Brassica cauliflora, Chou fleur,
Käse-Kohl.

truncated tower of the Désert de Retz. It was crammed with ruined furniture.
Should I laugh at their skeletons or fear that one of life's baleful remnants…

    The sudden shattering of a windowpane made me shudder, and
decided it: a vegetable arm, crooked, twisted, in which I had no difficulty
recognizing the workings, the surreptitious approach, the reptilian mind
of the wistaria, had just struck, broken, and entered.

Vincent van Gogh

PAINT YOUR GARDEN AS IT IS

*To Emile Bernard, St. Rémy, 188_*

 S YOU KNOW, once or twice, while Gauguin was in Arles, I gave myself free rein with abstractions, for instance in the "Woman Rocking," in the "Woman Reading a Novel," black in a yellow library; and at the time abstraction seemed to me a charming path. But it is enchanted ground, old man, and one soon finds oneself up against a stone wall.

I won't say that one might not venture on it after a virile lifetime of

GEORGE BROOKSHAW

{A Collection of the Most Esteemed Fruits}

Muscus clav-tus pro, *Ricinus maior.*
cubens

BASIL BESLER

{Hortus Eystettensis}

research, of a hand-to-hand struggle with nature, but I personally don't want to bother my head with such things. I have been slaving away on nature the whole year, hardly thinking of Impressionism or of this, that, and the other. And yet, once again I let myself go reaching for stars that are too big—a new failure—and I have had enough of it.

So I am working at present among the olive trees, seeking after the various effects of a gray sky against a yellow soil, with a green-black note in the foliage; another time the soil and the foliage all of a violet hue against a yellow sky; then again a red-ocher soil and a pinkish green sky. Yes, certainly, this interests me far more than the above-mentioned abstractions.

If I have not written you for a long while, it is because, as I had to struggle against my illness, I hardly felt inclined to enter into discussions— and I found danger in these abstractions. If I work on very quietly, the beautiful subjects will come of their own accord; really, above all, the great thing is to gather new vigor in reality, without any preconceived plan of Parisian prejudice....

I am telling you about these two canvases, especially about the first one, to remind you that one can try to give an impression of anguish without aiming straight at the historic Garden of Gethsemane; that it is not necessary to portray the characters of the Sermon on the Mount in order to produce a consoling and gentle motif.

Oh! undoubtedly it is wise and proper to be moved by the Bible, but modern reality has got such a hold on us that, even when we attempt to reconstruct the ancient days in our thoughts abstractly, the minor events of our lives tear us away from our meditations, and our own adventures thrust us back into our personal sensations—joy, boredom, suffering, anger, or a smile....

SOMETIMES BY ERRING one finds the right road. Go make up for it by painting your garden just as it is, or whatever you like. In any case it is a good thing to seek for distinction, nobility in the figures; and studies represent a real effort, and consequently something quite different from a waste of time. Being able to divide a canvas into great planes which intermingle, to find lines, forms which make contrasts, that is technique, tricks if you like, cuisine, but it is a sign all the same that you are studying your handicraft more deeply, and that is a good thing.

However hateful painting may be, and however cumbersome in the times we are living in, if anyone who has chosen this handicraft pursues it zealously, he is a man of duty, sound and faithful. Society makes our existence wretchedly difficult at times, hence our impotence and the imperfection of our work. I believe that even Gauguin himself suffers greatly under it too, and cannot develop his powers, although it is in him to do it. I myself am suffering under an absolute lack of models. But on the other hand there are beautiful spots here. I have just done five size 30 canvases, olive trees. And the reason I am staying on here is that my health is improving a great deal. What I am doing is hard, dry, but that is because I am trying to gather new strength by doing some rough work, and I'm afraid abstractions would make me soft.

Diodorus

THE HANGING
GARDENS OF BABYLON

 HERE WAS ... the Hanging Garden, as it is called, which was built, not by Semiramis, but by a later Syrian king to please one of his concubines; for she, they say, being a Persian by race and longing for the meadows of her mountains, asked the king to imitate, through the artifice of a planted garden, the distinctive landscape of Persia. The park extended four plethra on each side and since the approach to the garden sloped like a hillside and the several parts of the structure rose from one another tier on tier, the appearance of the whole resembled that of a theatre. When the ascending terraces had been built,

The Blue Egyptian Water Lily

London. Published Sept.r 1 1804, by Dr. Thornton.

DR. ROBERT JOHN THORNTON

{The Temple of Flora}

there had been constructed beneath them galleries which carried the entire weight of the planted garden and rose little by little one above the other along the approach; and the uppermost gallery, which was fifty cubits high, bore the highest surface of the park, which was made level with the circuit wall of the battlements of the city. Furthermore, the walls, which had been constructed at great expense, were twenty-two feet thick, while the passage-way between each two walls was ten feet wide. The roofs of the galleries were covered over with beams of stone sixteen feet long, inclusive of the overlap, and four feet wide. The roof above these beams had first a layer of reeds laid in great quantities of bitumen, over this two courses of baked brick bonded by cement, and as a third layer a covering of lead, to the end that the moisture from the soil might not penetrate beneath. On all this again earth had been piled to a depth sufficient for the roots of the largest trees; and the ground, when levelled off, was thickly planted with trees of every kind that, by their great size or any other charm, could give pleasure to the beholder. And since the galleries, each projecting beyond another, all received the light, they contained many royal lodgings of every description; and there was one gallery which contained openings leading from the topmost surface and machines for supplying the garden with water, the machines raising the water in great abundance from the river, although no one outside could see it being done. Now this park, as I have said, was a later construction.

Sylvia Plath

MUSHROOMS

VERNIGHT, VERY

Whitely, discreetly,

Very quietly

Our toes, our noses

Take hold on the loam,

Acquire the air.

Piper Indicum maxi,
mum longum.

Piper Indicum minus
recurvis siliquis.

BASIL BESLER

{Hortus Eystettensis}

Nobody sees us,

Stops us, betrays us;

The small grains make room.

Soft fists insist on

Heaving the needles,

The leafy bedding,

Even the paving.

Our hammers, our rams,

Earless and eyeless,

Perfectly voiceless,

Widen the crannies,

Shoulder through holes. We

Diet on water,

On crumbs of shadow,

Bland-mannered, asking

Little or nothing.

So many of us!

So many of us!

We are shelves, we are

Tables, we are meek,

We are edible,

Nudgers and shovers

In spite of ourselves.

Our kind multiplies:

We shall by morning

Inherit the earth.

Our foot's in the door.

Thomas Jefferson

GARDEN BOOK

{JEFFERSON TO CHARLES WILLSON PEALE}

Poplar Forest, August 20, 1811

HAVE OFTEN THOUGHT that if heaven had given me choice of my position and calling, it should have been on a rich spot of earth, well watered, and near a good market for the productions of the garden. No occupation is so delightful to me as the culture of the earth, and no culture comparable to that of the

Piper minimum Siliquis rotundis.

Piper Indicum rotundium maximum.

BASIL BESLER

{Hortus Eystettensis}

garden. Such a variety of subjects, some one always comming to perfection, the failure of one thing repaired by the success of another, and instead of one harvest a continued one through the year. Under a total want of demand except for our family table, I am still devoted to the garden. But though an old man, I am but a young gardener

Fontainebleau, Oct. 28, 1785.

To Reverend James Madison,

...After descending the hill again I saw a man cutting fern. I went to him under pretence of asking the shortest road to town, and afterwards asked for what use he was cutting fern. He told me that this part of the country furnished a great deal of fruit to Paris. That when packed in straw it acquired an ill taste, but that dry fern preserved it perfectly without communicating any taste at all.

I treasured this observation for the preservation of my apples on my return to my own country. They have no apples here to compare with our *Redtown* pippin. They have nothing which deserves the name of a peach; there being not sun enough to ripen the plum-peach and the best of their soft peaches being like our autumn peaches. Their cherries and strawberries are fair, but I think lack flavor. Their plums I think are better; so also their gooseberries, and the pears infinitely beyond any thing we possess. They have nothing better than our sweet-water; but they have a succession of as good from early in the summer till frost.

I am tomorrow to get (to) M. Malsherbes (an uncle of the Chevalier Luzerne's) about seven leagues from hence, who is the most curious man in France as to his trees. He is making for me a collection of the vines from which the Burgundy, Champagne, Bordeaux, Frontignac, and other of the most valuable wines of this country are made. Another gentleman is collecting for me the best eating grapes, including what we call the raisin. I propose also to endeavor to colonize their hare, rabbit, red and gray partridge, pheasants of different kinds, and some other birds....

{JEFFERSON TO MARIA JEFFERSON}

New York, June 13th, 1790.

...We had not peas nor strawberries here till the 8th day of this month. On the same day I heard the first whip-poor-will whistle. Swallows and martins appeared here on the 21st of April. When did they appear with you? and when had you peas, strawberries, and whip-poor-wills in Virginia? Take notice hereafter whether the whip-poor-wills always come with the strawberries and peas....

{JEFFERSON TO SAMUEL VAUGHAN, JR.}

Philadelphia Nov. 27. 1790.

We have lately had introduced a plant of the melon species which from it's external resemblance to the pumpkin, we have called a pumpkin, distinguishing it specifically as the potatoe-pumpkin, on account of the extreme resemblance of its taste to that of the sweet-potatoe. it is as yet but little known, is well esteemed at our tables, and particularly valued by our negroes. coming much earlier than the real potatoe, we are so much the

sooner furnished with a substitute for that root. I know not from whence
it came; so that perhaps it may be originally from your islands. in that case
you will only have the trouble of throwing away the few seeds I enclose
you herewith. on the other hand, if unknown to you, I think it will
probably succeed in the islands, and may add to the catalogue of plants
which will do as substitutes for bread. I have always thought that if in the
experiments to introduce or to communicate new plants, one species in a
hundred is found useful and succeeds, the ninety nine found otherwise
are more than paid for.

{JEFFERSON TO MARIA JEFFERSON}
Philadelphia, Mar. 9th, 1791.

...On the 27th of February I saw blackbirds and robin-red breasts, and on
the 7th of this month I heard frogs for the first time this year. Have you
noted the first appearance of these things at Monticello? I hope you have,
and will continue to note every appearance, animal and vegetable, which
indicates the approach of spring, and will communicate them to me.

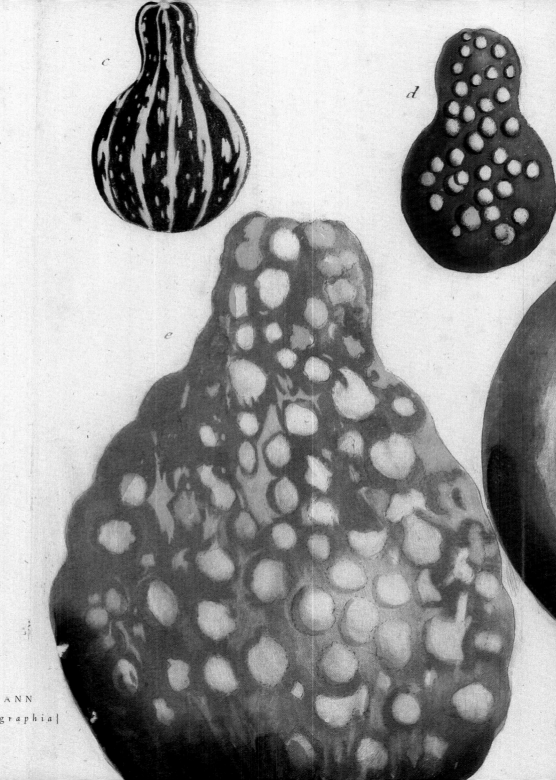

JOHANN WEINMANN
{Phytanthoza Iconographia}
Detail

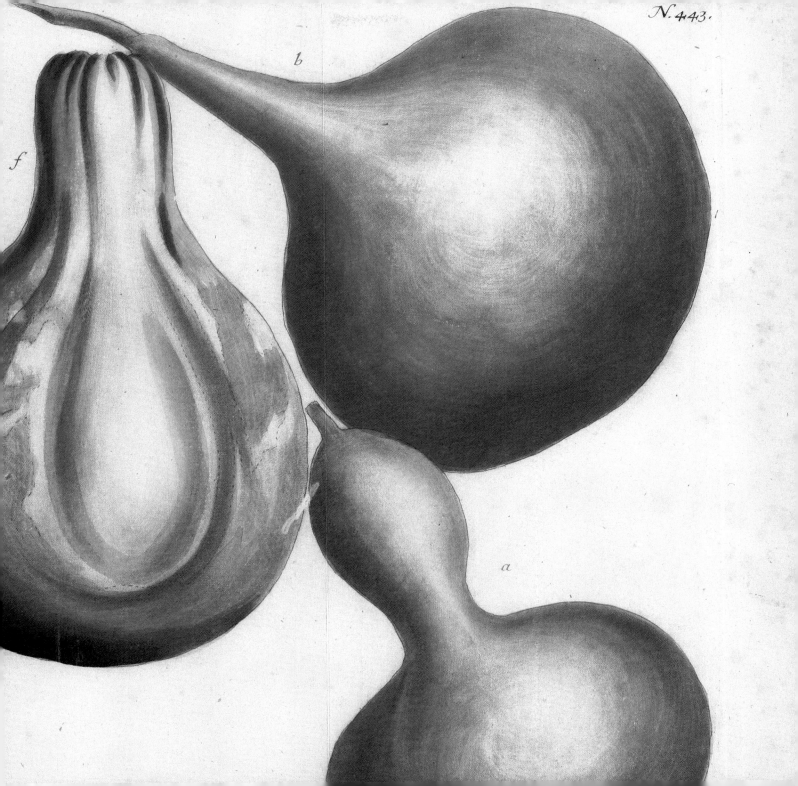

By these means we shall be able to compare the climates of Philadelphia and Monticello. Tell me when you shall have peas, etc, up: when everything comes to table: when you shall have the first chickens hatched; when every kind of tree blossoms, or puts forth leaves; when each kind of flower blooms...

{JEFFERSON TO WILLIAM DRAYTON}

Philadelphia May 1. 1791.

my Mortification has been extreme at the delays which have attended the procuring the olive plants so long ago recommended by myself, so long ago agreed to by the agricultural society, & for which their money has been so long lying in the hands of a banker at Paris I assure you Sir that my endeavors have been unremitting. in addition to the first small parcel which were sent soon after the receipt of your orders, I have now the pleasure to inform you that a second cargo is arrived at Baltimore consisting of 6. barrels which contain 40. young olive trees of the best species, to afford grafts, and a box of olives to sow for stocks. this I order on immediately to Charleston to care of Messrs. Brailsford & Morris for you, and I inclose herewith a copy of the directions given for the manner of treating them. a third cargo is on it's way from Bordeaux, but for what port I have not learned. this consists of 2. barrels containing 44. olive trees of which 24 are very young.—I shall immediately write to my correspondent at Marseilles to send another cargo the ensuing winter.—I delivered to m͞r Izard a barrel of Mountain rice of last year's growth, which I received from the island of Bananas on the coast of Africa & which I desired him to share with you for the use of the society. the attention now paying to the sugar-maple tree promises us an abundant supply of sugar at home: and I confess I look with infinite gratification to the addition to the products of the U.S. of three such articles as oil, sugar, & upland rice. the last I value, in the hopes it may be a complete substitute for the pestiferous culture of the wet rice....

Memorandum for the Olive Trees

If the olive trees arrive safely on the ground where they are intended to be planted, before the end of the month of May next, they may yet be planted one foot depth in the earth above the root & from 15 to 18 feet distance one from the other in a Square. If on the contrary they arrive after the month of May, they will open a trench in the earth of the depth of the barrels in which they will place the barrels near each other, taking out the hoops and 3 or 4 staves and filling the hole all round with earth. They will water 3 or 4 times in summer all the trench 'till the water penetrates below the bottoms of the barrels. They will shade them from the sun during the great heats & in convenient season they will be planted as above.

As for the chest of olives for sowing. They will make a hole of 3 feet depth in the earth put the chest in it, as it is, cover it over with the same earth and water it well afterwards. They will then leave the whole so 'till next February, when they will uncover the chest without deranging it & take some of the Olives which they will break to see if the almond has germinated; if it has not yet swelled they will cover it again & leave it for one year more. If they have swelled they will sow them at an inch depth in the earth cover them again with earth & put on them horse dung one inch watering them with a watering pot then they will sprout out in 2 or 3 months or perhaps not till the ensuing year.

{JEFFERSON TO GENERAL HENRY KNOX}

Monticello June 1. 1795.

...have you become a farmer? is it not pleasanter than to be shut up within 4.
walls and delving eternally with the pen? I am become the most ardent
farmer in the state. I live on my horse from morning to night almost. intervals
are filled up with attentions to a nailery I carry on. I rarely look into a book,
and more rarely take up a pen. I have proscribed newspapers. not taking a single one, nor scarcely ever looking into one. my next reformation will be to
allow neither pen, ink, nor paper to be kept on the farm. when I have accom-
plished this I shall be in a fair way of indemnifying myself for the drudgery
in which I have passed my life. if you are half as much delighted with the
farm as I am, you bless your stars at your riddance from public cares....

{JEFFERSON TO JAMES MAURY}

Washington July 1. 06.

...We have been lately alarmed with the appearance of a caterpillar which
at first threatened destruction to our small grain, Indian corn, tobacco &

Painted by P.R.A. pinxt.   Cooking's Eclipse   Primrose   Sutherland sculpt.

A Group of Auriculas.

Pub.d as the Act directs by Dr Thornton May 1, 1803

grasses. it has happily however disappeared after little injury. we are now

gathering in one of the most plentiful harvests we have ever known. of

tobacco there has not been plants enough to put in half a crop. this pro-

ceeded from the drought of the spring....

{JOHN P. VAN NESS TO JEFFERSON}

July 5, 1806

I take the liberty of sending you by the Bearer two worms which I took

this afternoon on a lombardy poplar tree standing on dry ground,

that answers, I think, very well (although the colour of the same worm

is variegated and the shades of the two are different from each other)

the description of the reptile, said to be poisenous, which infests these

ornamental trees. As this subject has lately excited some speculation, I

supposed it would be gratifying to you to observe the worm particularly;

and therefore trouble you with this communication which I beg you will

be so obliging as to excuse.

{JEFFERSON TO TIMOTHY MATLACK}

Washington Oct. 19. 07.

I duly received your present of Sickel's pears, most of them in their highest

point of perfection, two or three just past it. they exceeded anything I have

tasted since I left France, & equalled any pear I had seen there. they

renewed my regrets for the loss of the last spring. the bundle of trees you so

kindly sent me, were longer coming here than they should have been, but

going hence to Monticello in a cart, they were out in the remarkable severe

weather we had in the middle & latter part of March, and by the impass-

ableness of the roads & breaking down of the cart were so long out that not

a single one survived. I will not trouble you with a new request until I go

home myself to remain, which will be on the 4th of March after next. but if

in the February preceeding that (say Feb. 1809) you should have any

plants to spare of what you deem *excellent* pears, peaches, or grapes, they

will then be most acceptable indeed, and I shall be able to carry & plant

them myself at Monticello where I shall then begin to occupy myself

according to my own natural inclinations, which have been so long kept down by the history of our times; and shall bid a joyful adieu to politics

and all the odious passions & vices of which they make us the object in

public life. I should be very much pleased to see you at Monticello & to

prove to you that my heart has been always there, altho my body has been

every where, except there, since our first acquaintance in 1775....

{JEFFERSON TO BERNARD MCMAHON}

Monticello Apr. 8. 11.

I have been long wishing for an opportunity, by someone going to

Philadelphia in the stage, to take charge of a packet of seeds for you. it is

too large to trespass on the post-mail. I received them from my old friend

Thouin, director of the National garden of France. but the advance of the

season obliges me to confide them to a gentleman going no further than

Washington, there to look out for some one going on to Philadelphia. I

have added to them a dozen genuine Glocester hiccory nuts of the last

season sent me from the place of their growth. your favor of the 10th ulo came safe to hand with the seeds, for which accept my thanks. you enquire whether I have a hot house, greenhouse, or to what extent I pay attention to these things. I have only a green house, and have used that only for a very few articles. my frequent & long absences at a distant possession render my efforts even for the few greenhouse plants I aim at, abortive. during my last absence in the winter, every plant I had in it perished. I have an extensive flower border, in which I am fond of placing *handsome* plants or *fragrant*. those of mere curiosity I do not aim at, having too many other cares to bestow more than a moderate attention to them. in this I have placed the seeds you were so kind as to send me last. in it I have also growing the fine tulips, hyacinths, tuberoses & Amaryllis you formerly sent me. my wants there are Anemones, Auriculas, Ranunculus, Crown Imperials & Carnations: in the garden your fine gooseberries, Hudson & Chili strawberries: some handsome lillies. but the season is now too far advanced. during the next season they will be acceptable. small parcels of seed may come by post; but bulbs are too bulky. We have always medical students in Philadelphia coming home by the stage when their lectures cease in the fall who would take charge of small packages, or they may

come at any time by vessels bound to Richmond, addressed to the care of

Messrs Gibson & Jefferson. I have put into your packet some Benni seed.

we now raise it and make from it our own sallad oil preferable to such

olive oil as is usually to be bought....

{JEFFERSON TO GEORGE DIVERS}

Monticello Mar. 1 0. 1 2.

I promised to stock you with the Alpine strawberry as soon as my beds

would permit. I now send you a basket of plants and can spare you 10.

baskets more if you desire it. their value, you know, is the giving strawberries

8. months in the year. but they require a large piece of ground and therefore

I am moving them into the truck patch, as I cannot afford them room

enough in the garden. I have received from McMahon some plants of the

true Hudson strawberry. the last rains have brought them forward and

ensured their living. I have been 20 years trying unsuccessfully to get them here. the next year I shall be able to stock you. I have received also

from McMahon 4. plants of his wonderful gooseberry. I measured the fruit

of them 3. I. round. by the next year I hope they will afford you cuttings.

about 20. plants of the Sprout kale have given us sprouts from the 1st of

December. their second growth now furnishes us a dish nearly every day,

and they will enable me this year to stock my neighbors with the seed. we

have now got the famous Irish grass, Fiorin, ensured and growing. they

make hay from it in December, January, February. I received the plants

from Ireland about a month ago. I am now engaged in planting a collection

of pears. I know you have several kinds of very fine. if your nursery can

spare 2. of each kind I will thank you for them: if not then some cuttings

for engrafting, tying up each separately....

{JEFFERSON TO WILLIAM JOHNSON}

Monticello May 10. 17.

...the pamphlet you were so kind as to send me manifests a zeal, which

cannot be too much praised, for the interests of agriculture, the

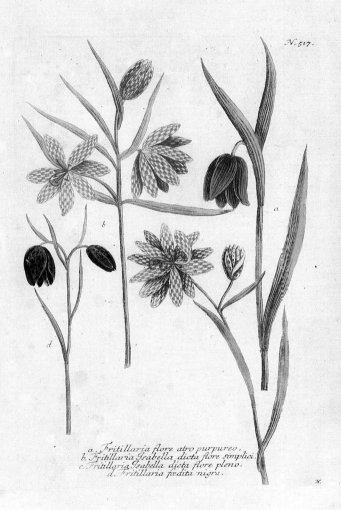

a. *Fritillaria flore atro purpureo.*
b. *Fritillaria Isabella dicta flore simplici.*
c. *Fritillaria Isabella dicta flore pleno.*
d. *Fritillaria fœdita nigra.*

JOHANN WEINMANN

{P h y t a n t h o z a   I c o n o g r a p h i a}

employment of our first parents in Eden, the happiest we can follow,
and the most important to our country. while it displays the happy
capabilities of that portion of it which you inhabit, it shews how much
is yet to be done to develop them fully. I am not without hope that thro'
your efforts and example, we shall yet see it a country abounding in
wine and oil. North Carolina has the merit of taking the lead in the former
culture, of giving the first specimen of an exquisite wine, produced in
quantity, and established in it's culture beyond the danger of being
discontinued. her Scuppernon wine, made on the Southside of the
Sound, would be distinguished on the best tables of Europe, for it's fine
aroma, and chrystalline transparence. unhappily that aroma, in most of
the samples I have seen, has been entirely submerged in brandy. this
coarse taste and practice is the peculiarity of Englishmen, and of their
apes Americans. I hope it will be discontinued, and that this fortunate
example will encourage our country to go forward in this culture. the
olive, the Sesamus, the Cane & Coffee offer field enough for the efforts
of your's and other states South & West of you. we, of this state, must

make bread, and be contented with so much of that as a miserable insect
will leave us. this remnant will scarcely feed us the present year, for
such swarms of the Wheat-fly were never before seen in this country....

{JEFFERSON TO SAMUEL MAVERICK}

South Carolina, May 12. 22.

Age, debility and decay of memory have for some time withdrawn me
from attention to matters without doors. the grape you inquire after as
having gone from this place is not now recollected by me. as some in my
vineyard have died, others have been substituted without noting which,
so that at present all are unknown. that as good wines will be made in
America as in Europe the Scuppernon of North Carolina furnishes
sufficient proof. the vine is congenial to every climate in Europe from
Hungary to the Mediterranean, and will be bound to succeed in the same
temperatures here wherever tried by intelligent vignerons. the culture
however is more desirable for domestic use than profitable as an
occupation for market. in countries which use ardent spirits drunkenness

is the mortal vice; but in those which make wine for common use you never see a drunkard.

{JEFFERSON TO THOMAS WORTHINGTON}

Monticello, Nov. 29. 25.

You will startle at the receipt of this letter as if it were from the dead; and indeed the ordinary term of man's life says I ought to have been so sometime. however, here I am as yet, not in very good health indeed, but as good perhaps as I ought to expect; and avail myself of a little circumstance to take occasion to recall myself to your recollection. I have pasted the text of my letter at it's head. but texts cut out of a newspaper are not like those of holy writ, articles of faith. and the object of my letter is to ask you if this text is really true? and if it is to request further that you will procure for me and send in a letter by mail half a dozen seeds of these mammoth cucumbers. one of 4 f. 6 i long, and another of 4 f. 5 ³⁄₄ should afford so many seeds as to spare a few to a beggar. altho giants do not always beget giants, yet I should count on their improving the breed, and this vegetable being a great favorite of mine, I wish to take the chance of an improvement. but whether successful or not I shall find my reward in the occasion it furnishes of recalling myself to your recollection and of assuring you of my constant esteem and respect.

Raymond Carver

HOMINY AND RAIN

 N A LITTLE patch of ground beside
the wall of the Earth Sciences building,
a man in a canvas hat was on
his knees doing something in the rain
with some plants. Piano music
came from an upstairs window
in the building next door. Then
the music stopped.
And the window was brought down.

PLATE XC
Published by G. Brookshaw from the place this day by M. the Author 1 Nov. 1 Lambeth 1812

Chondrilla Serinoides dicta cœrulea Tanacetum inodorum flore Belli Calendula flore simplici
flore completo.   dis maioris.

You told me those white blossoms
on the cherry trees in the Quad
smelled like a can of just-opened
hominy. Hominy. They reminded you
of that. This may or may not
be true. I can't say.
I've lost my sense of smell,
along with any interest I may ever
have expressed in working
on my knees with plants, or
vegetables. There was a barefoot

madman with a ring in his ear
playing his guitar and singing
reggae. I remember that.
Rain puddling around his feet.
The place he'd picked to stand
had Welcome Fear
painted on the sidewalk in red letters.

At the time it seemed important
to recall the man on his knees
in front of his plants.
The blossoms. Music of one kind,
and another. Now I'm not so sure.
I can't say, for sure.

It's a little like some tiny cave-in,
in my brain. There's a sense
that I've lost—not everything,
not everything, but far too much.
A part of my life forever.
Like hominy.

Even though your arm stayed linked
in mine. Even though that. Even
though we stood quietly in the
doorway as the rain picked up.
And watched it without saying

anything. Stood quietly.

At peace, I think. Stood watching

the rain. While the one

with the guitar played on.

Geoffrey Chaucer

THE BOOK
OF THE DUCHESS

 WAS GO WALKED fro my tree,
And as I wente, ther cam by mee
A whelp, that fauned me as I stood,
That hadde yfolowed, and koude no good.

Hyt com and crepte to me as lowe
Rygh: as hyt hadde me yknowe
Helde doun hys hed and joyned hys eres,
Anc leyde al smothe doun hys heres.
I welde have kaught hyt, and anoon
Hyt fledde, and was fro me goon;
And I hym folwed, and hyt forth wente
Doun by a floury grene wente

a. *Convolvulus pennatus Americanus, quamoclit,* Federwinde.
b. *Convolvulus peregrinus flore rubro hederæ folio.*

JOHANN WEINMANN

{Phytanthoza Iconographia}

Ful thikke of gras, ful softe and swete.

With floures fele, faire under fete,

And litel used, hyt semed thus;

For both Flora and Zephirus,

They two that make floures growe,

Had mad her dwellynge ther, I trowe;

For hit was, on to beholde,

As thogh the erthe envye wolde

To be gayer than the heven,

To have moo floures, swiche seven,

As in the welken sterres bee.

Hyt had forgete the povertee

That wynter, thorgh hys colde morwes,

Had mad hyt suffre, and his sorwes,

All was forgeten, and that was sene.

For al the woode was waxen grene;

Swetnesse of dew had mad hyt waxe.

    Hyt ys no nede eke for to axe

Wher there were many grene greves,

Or thikke of trees, so ful of leves

And every tree stood by hymselve

Fro other wel ten foot or twelve.

So grete trees, so huge of strengthe,

Of fourty or fifty fadme lengthe

Clene withoute bowgh or stikke,

With croppes brode, and eke as thikke—

They were nat an ynche asonder—

That hit was shadewe overal under.

And many an hert and many an hynde

Was both before me and behynde.

Of founes, sowres, bukkes, does

Was ful the woode, and many roes,

And many sqwirelles, that sete

Ful high upon the trees and ete,

And in hir maner made festes.

Shortly, hyt was so ful of bestes,

That thogh Argus, the noble countour,

Sete to rekene in hys countour,

And rekened with his figures ten—

For by tho figures mowe al ken

Yf they be crafty, rekene and noumbre,

And telle of every thing the noumbre—

Yet shoulde he fayle to rekene even

The wondres me mette in my sweven.

Frances Hodgson Burnett

THE SECRET GARDEN

 ARY HAD STEPPED close to the robin, and suddenly the gust of wind swung aside some loose ivy trails, and more suddenly still she jumped towards them and caught them in her hand. This she did because she had seen something under them— a round knob which had been covered by the leaves hanging over it. It was the knob of a door.

She put her hands under the leaves and began to pull and push them aside. Thick as the ivy hung, it nearly all was a loose and swinging curtain, though some had crept over wood and iron. Mary's heart began to

The Nodding Rencalmia

London Published Nov.r 1 1804 by D.r Thornton

Alt.enderson pinxel.   Caldwall sculpt.

DR. ROBERT JOHN THORNTON

{The Temple of Flora}

thump and her hands to shake a little in her delight and excitement. The robin kept singing and twittering away and tilting his head on one side, as if he were as excited as she was. What was this under her hands which was square and made of iron and which her fingers found a hole in?

It was the lock of the door which had been closed ten years, and she put her hand in her pocket, drew out the key, and found it fitted the keyhole. She put the key in and turned it. It took two hands to do it, but it did turn.

And then she took a long breath and looked behind her up the long walk to see if anyone was coming. No one was coming. No one ever did come, it seemed, and she took another long breath, because she could not help it, and she held back the swinging curtain of ivy and pushed back the door which opened slowly—slowly.

Then she slipped through it, and shut it behind her, and stood with her back against it, looking about her and breathing quite fast with excitement, and wonder, and delight.

She was standing *inside* the secret garden.

It was the sweetest, most mysterious-looking place anyone could imagine. The high walls which shut it in were covered with the leafless stems of climbing roses, which were so thick that they were matted together. Mary Lennox knew they were roses because she had seen a great many roses in India. All the ground was covered with grass of wintry brown, and out of it grew clumps of bushes which were surely rose-bushes if they were alive. There were numbers of standard roses which had so spread their branches that they were like little trees. There were other trees in the garden, and one of the things that made the place look strangest and loveliest was that climbing roses had run all over them and swung down long tendrils which made light swaying curtains, and here and there they had caught at each other or at a far-reaching branch and had crept from one tree to another and made lovely bridges of themselves. There were neither leaves nor roses on them now, and Mary did not know whether they were dead or alive, but their thin grey or brown branches and sprays looked like a sort of hazy mantle spreading over everything, walls, and trees, and even brown grass, where they had fallen from their fastenings and run along the ground. It was this hazy tangle from tree to tree which made it look so mysterious. Mary had thought it must be different from other gardens which had not been left all by themselves so long; and, indeed, it was different from any other place she had ever seen in her life.

'How still it is!' she whispered. 'How still!'

Then she waited a moment and listened at the stillness. The robin, who had flown to his tree-top, was still as all the rest. He did not even flutter his wings; he sat without stirring and looked at Mary.

'No wonder it is still,' she whispered again, 'I am the first person who has spoken in here for ten years.'

She moved away from the door, stepping as softly as if she were afraid of awakening someone. She was glad that there was grass under her feet and that her steps made no sounds. She walked under one of the fairy-like arches between the trees and looked up at the tendrils and sprays which formed them.

'I wonder if they are all quite dead,' she said. 'Is it all a quite dead garden? I wish it wasn't.' …

But she was *inside* the wonderful garden, and she could come through the door under the ivy at any time, and she felt she had found a world all her own.

The sun was shining inside the four walls and the high arch of blue sky over this particular piece of Misselthwaite seemed even more brilliant and soft than it was over the moor. The robin flew down from his tree-top and hopped about or flew after her from one bush to another. He chirped a good deal and had a very busy air, as if he were showing her things.

Everything was strange and silent, and she seemed to be hundreds of miles away from anyone, but somehow she did not feel lonely at all. All that troubled her was her wish that she knew whether all the roses were dead, or if perhaps some of them had lived and might put out leaves and buds as the weather got warmer. She did not want it to be a quite dead garden. If it were a quite alive garden, how wonderful it would be, and what thousands of roses would grow on every side!

Her skipping-rope had hung over her arm when she came in, and after she had walked about for a while she thought she would skip round the whole garden, stopping when she wanted to look at things. There seemed to have been grass paths here and there, and in one or two corners there were alcoves of ever-green with stone seats or tall moss-covered flower-urns in them.

As she came near the second of these alcoves she stopped skipping. There had once been a flower-bed in it, and she thought she saw something sticking out of the black earth—some sharp little pale green points. She remembered what Ben Weatherstaff had said, and she knelt down to look at them.

'Yes, they are tiny growing things and they *might* be crocuses or snowdrops or daffodils,' she whispered.

She bent very close to them and sniffed the fresh scent of the damp earth....

Thomas Hill

THE GARDENER'S LABYRINTH

THE GARDEN RADISH with us, is better knowne, then I with pen can utter the discription of the same, for in a manner every person as well, as well the rich as the poore, the Citizens as Countrimen, when their stomack is slack or irketh at meat: they then to procure an appetite to feeding, by the same root, by cutting the roots either into a length on each side, or into round slyces, doe workmanlike season them with salt, heating them for the more delight in the mouth, between two dishes, supposing a more tendernesse caused to the roots, through the like doing: whose care and diligence in the

Hyacinthus Stellatus
flore coeruleo:

Arum latifolium:

Arum:

Colchicum Vernum
flo pleno purpureum:

BASIL BESLER

{Hortus Eystettensis}

bestowing of it in the earth, ought, (after the mind of *Columella*) to be after this manner; that the beds, before the bestowing of the seeds, be well laboured, and workmanlike turned in with dung, and when the roots be grown to some bignesse, then the earth to be raised and diligently heaped about them, for the roots shall be naked or lie bare of earth, that both the Sun and ayre beat upon them, then will they become in their further growth, both hard and hollow like to the Mushrome, as *Plinie* reporteth, which prescribeth to these both a loose and moist earth.

The worthy *Rutilius* (in his instructions of husbandrie) uttereth, that the Radishes refuse a hard, sandy, and gravelly ground, and do joy in the moisture of the aire: besides, these ought to be sown in beds a good distance asunder, and the earth deepe digged after a late or new rain fallen, except the place by hap shall be moist, and soon watered.

The seeds committed to the earth, ought immediately and with diligence, to be covered light with a Rake, and neither dung bestowed within, nor strewed upon the beds (although *Columella* otherwise willeth) but onely chaffe of Corne, as after shall further be uttered.

The skillful practised in Garden matters report, that these better prosper being orderly set, then curiously sowne, and that these to be bestowed in the earth, as both sown and set, at two times of the yeare, as in the moneth of February, and beginning of March, if the owner shall enjoy the roots timely, and in August unto the middest of September, if the owner would enjoy them much sooner: and these then bestowed in the earth, are without doubt far better, forasmuch as the Radish in the cold season, groweth and encreaseth especially in the root, and is the same time tenderer, whereas the plants otherwise in the faire and warm season, runne up into a leafe or stem. Yet this manner of tryall, to possesse them in sharp Winter, is little use with us, because the Radish can ill abide the bitter ayre, which once bitten and tainted with the frosts either therewith, or soon after dyeth: yet the learned *Plinie* writing of the Radish, uttereth the same to joy so much in the cold ayre, that in Germany hath sometimes been seen a Radish, which grew in compasse so big as an infants middle.

The skilful *Aristomachus* in his learned instructions of husbandry, willeth that the leaves of the Radish in the winter time be broken off, and thrown away, and to heape the earth high about them, least puddles of water do stand in the beds, for the roots on such wise increase and be big in summer time.

Howsoever the roots shal be handled, certain it is, that the cold ayre and frosts do increase and sweeten the roots (as afore uttered of the Rape) if so be they may continue in winter time: for the cold ayre converteth the increasment into the roots, and not into the leaves, although that those (as *Theophrastus* uttereth) doe wax then hard in many places.

The roots are caused to grow the sweeter in eating, and more delectable in taste, if the leaves be broken off (as *Pliny* hath noted) before the Radishes shoot up into a stem.

And the leaf of the Radish, how much the smaller the same shall be, even so much the tenderer and delectable root will it yield, which by watering with a salt liquor, or pickle, causeth to breath forth the bitternesse quite, if any such rest or be in the root.

As the like *Pliny* wrote, that the Radish is to be fed, yea and willed the roots for the tendernesse, to be often watered with pickle, or salt water.

The Egyptians watered with Nitre, to the end the roots might be commendable in sweetnesse and delight to the mouth, which possesse a Cartilage and thick, rinde: to these, in many roots, sharp in taste, yet delectable in the eating, which are part left bare above the ground becometh tough and hard, through the occasion afore uttered, and hollow (like to the Mushroom) unlesse they be wel covered about with light earth.

There are Radishes supposed to be of a feminine kind, which be so sharp, and these possesse smaller leaves, and to the eye be a fairer green, as *Rutilius* writeth.

If the owner covet to enjoy sweet roots in tast, then after the counsell and mind of the singular *Florentine*, let him steep the seeds for two dayes before, in either water or hony, or Cuite, or else sugred water, and these dried in the shadow, to commit them orderly to the earth.

If the Gardener desire to possesse faire and great roots, let him (after the mind of the aforesaid *Rutilius*) when the roots be grown to some bigness, pluck away all the leaves, saving two within to grow still, which done, cover the earth often over the heads to grow the sweeter and pleasanter.

A like experience in causing the root to become marvellous big, doth *Plinie* skilfully utter and teach, after this manner, by taking a great dibble, with the which making a hole in the earth wel six fingers deep, fill it up with fresh chaffe, after bestow a seed of the Radish with dung and light earth over the mouth, covering the same in like manner even with the earth; these performed, the root will grow and encrease unto the bignesse of the hole.

The skilful practitioners report, that the goodnesse of the Radish is

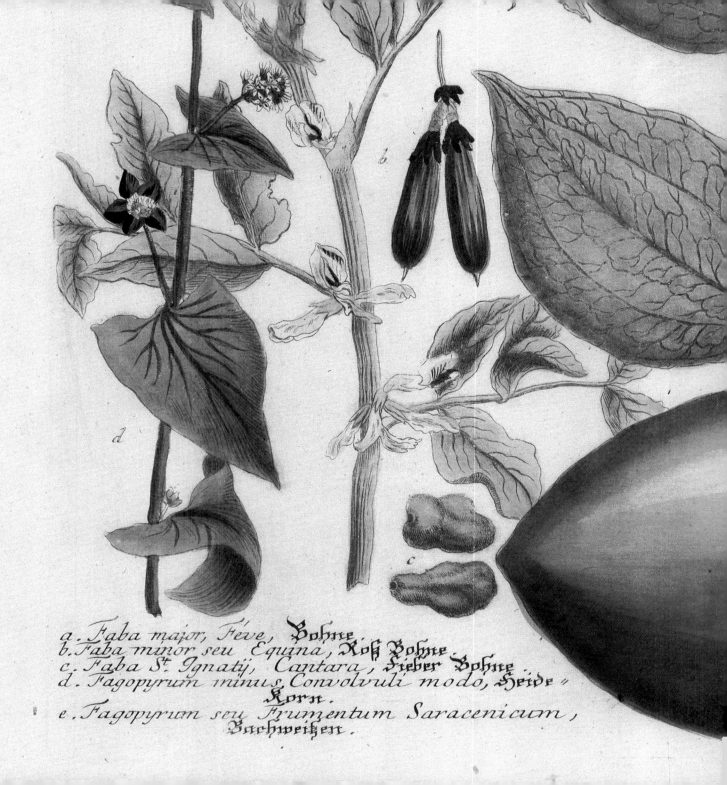

a. Faba major, Féve, Bohne
b. Faba minor seu Equina, Roß Bohne
c. Faba St. Ignatij, Cantara, Fieber Bohne
d. Fagopyrum minus, Convolvuli modo, Heide
Korn.
e. Fagopyrum seu Frumentum Saracenicum,
Buchweißen.

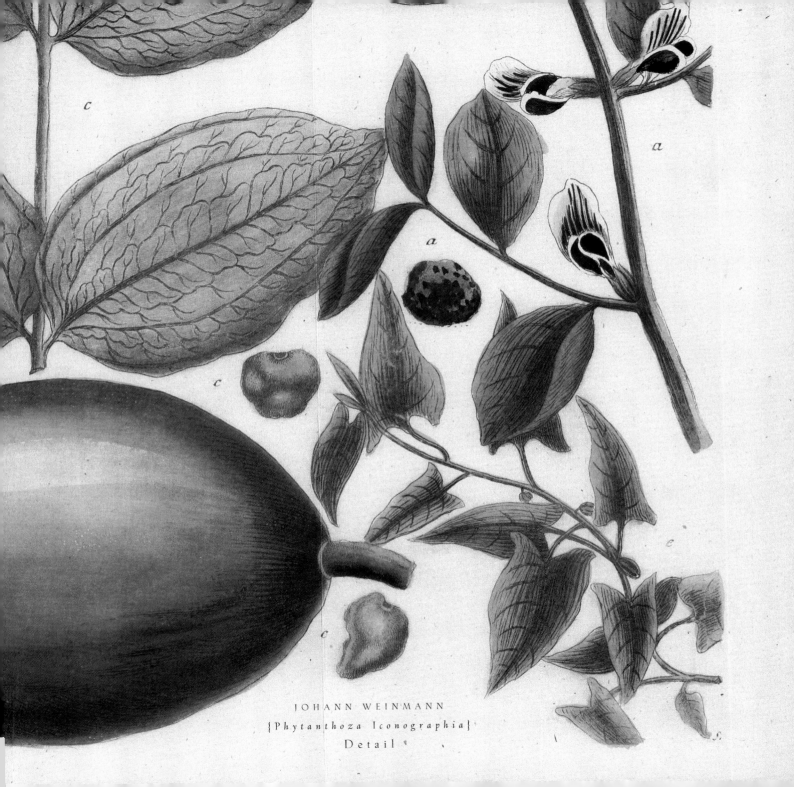

JOHANN WEINMANN

{Phytanthoza Iconographia}

Detail

known by the leaves, which the sweeter they be (after the manner) so much the tenderer and more pleasant are the roots in the eating: the like teacheth or sheweth the rinde, which the thinner the same is, so much the delectabler is the root in the tast of the mouth.

The thin bestowing of the seeds in well dressed beds, from the end of August unto the midst of September, and after the coming up diligently weeded about, with leaves broken off, the light earth covered about, and after watered with salt water, doe procure the roots not onely to wax, or grow the bigger, but tenderer and sweeter in the eating, forasmuch as the salt pickle very much abateth the bitternesse consisting in them, as by a like we customably see, that these be eaten with vinegar and salt.

And the plants better prosper, coming up in an open ayre, then bestowed in a shadowy place, where in the increase, the roots be much hindered.

If the owner happen to commit seeds to the earth in a drie season, let them be sown the thicker in beds, and if the same may be in a moist ground lightly watered.

The plants grown to a reasonable height above the earth, and that showres have moistened the ground a day before, the plants may then be removed, and set into beds wel laboured and workman-like dressed, which by diligence bestowed, grow the better and pleasanter in the eating.

That the Radish may not be harmed with the garden fleas, *Theophrastus* willeth to sow in the beds among them, the pulse named *Erum.*

Other singular helps for the most herbs, may be learned in my first part, which I have gathered for the most part out of ancient writers: Here is not to be overpassed, that in the Radishes a bitterness consisteth according to the thickness of the rinde, as the worthy *Pliny* uttereth, which writeth that these also do offend the teeth, by blunting or setting them on edge.

But in this place commeth to mind, a secret very profitable, and to be esteemed with Vinteners, which the Author freely uttereth to them.

If the Vintener cutteth a Radish into slices, and bestoweth those pieces into a vessel of corrupt Wine, doth in short time draw all the evil savour and lothsomnesse (if any consisteth in the wine) and to these the tartness of it like reviveth, which if the root be not able to rid and draw quite forth this default, let the same immediately be taken forth, and (if need shall require) put a fresh root like ordered. For this no doubt hath been proved, and profiteth many by understanding of this secret.

This no doubt is a secret very marvellous, that the Radish in no wise agreeth to be placed or grow nigh to the Vine, for the deadly hatred between them insomuch that the Vine neer growing, turneth or windeth back with the branches, as mightily disdaining and hating the Radish growing fast by if we may credit the learned *Plinie, Galen,* and the Neapolitane *Rutilius,* which seeme to have diligently noted the same.

And the reason they report to be like (as afore uttered of the agreement of the Colewort with wine) which is through the hid discord of natures consisting in them, so that if the places were changed, yet for all the removing, will they in no manner joy together.

Of which *Androcides* affirmeth the Radish and Colewort, to be a singular remedy against drunkenness, so that the ancient in Greece commonly joyned and matched the drinking of wine, with the Radish, as I afore uttered in the Chapter of the Colewort, so that no marvel it is if that these be used so common.

The Radish in time past hath been in much account, and so worthily esteemed, that *Moschion* the Greek wrote a large pamphlet of the worthy praises of the same yea the Radish before other meats, was so preferred in

Greece, that at *Delphos* in the temple of *Apollo*, the Radish was esteemed as Gold, the Beet as Silver and the Rape or Turnup as Lead.

The Radish also is said to polish very fair the Ivory, and buried in a heap of Salt, doth alter & reduce the same into a watry pickle.

The Radish to conclude, in the removing and setting again, looseth the sharpnesse resting in it, and this hath a singular delight in the rind, so that the same be new gathered and not too old of growth, therefore by the example of many seldome eaten, do unadvisedly refuse and omit the using of it.

And drawing to an end, I thinke it right profitable to utter the making of Vinegar with the Radish, as the learned *Petrus Cresoentius* (in his work of Husbandry) hath noted the same, the roots of the Radish (saith he) being dried and brought to fine pouder, and bestowed into a vessel which hath wine in it, let stand to settle (after the well labouring and mixing together) for certain daies: which done, the owner shall enjoy a Radish Vinegar, very laudable and much commended for the dissolving and wasting of the stone in the Kidneyes, and many other painfull griefs.

Helen Keller

THE SOUNDS
OF THE GARDEN

 LIVED, up to the time of the illness that deprived me of my sight and hearing, in a tiny house consisting of a large square room and a small one, in which the servant slept.

It is a custom in the South to build a small house near the homestead as an annex to be used on occasion. Such a house my father built after the Civil War, and when he married my mother they went to live in it. It was completely covered with vines, climbing roses and honeysuckles. From the garden it looked like an arbour. The little porch was hidden from view

by a screen of yellow roses and Southern similar. It was the favourite haunt of humming-birds and bees.

The Keller homestead, where the family lived, was a few steps from our little rose-bower. It was called "Ivy Green" because the house and the surrounding trees and fences were covered with beautiful English ivy. Its old-fashioned garden was the paradise of my childhood.

Even in the days before my teacher came, I used to feel along the square stiff boxwood hedges, and guided by the sense of smell, would find the first violets and lilies. There, too, after a fit of temper, I went to find comfort and to hide my hot face in the cool leaves and grass. What joy it was to lose myself in that garden of flowers, to wander happily from spot to spot, until, coming suddenly upon a beautiful vine, I recognized it by its leaves and blossoms, and knew it was the vine which covered the tumble-down summer-house at the farther end of the garden! Here, also, were trailing clematis, drooping jessamine, and some rare sweet flowers called butterfly lilies, because their fragile petals resemble butterflies' wings. But the roses—they were loveliest of all. Never have I found in the greenhouses of the North such heart-satisfying roses as the climbing roses of my southern home. They used to hang in long festoons from our porch, filling the whole air with their fragrance, untainted by any earthy smell; and in the early morning, washed in the dew, they felt so soft, so pure, I could not help wondering if they did not resemble the asphodels of God's garden.

I RECALL MANY incidents of the summer of 1887 that followed my soul's sudden awakening. I did nothing but explore with my hands and learn the name of every object that I touched; and the more I handled things and learned their names and uses, the more joyous and confident grew my sense of kinship with the rest of the world.

When the time of daisies and buttercups came Miss Sullivan took me by the hand across the fields, where men were preparing the earth for the seed, to the banks of the Tennessee River, and there, sitting on the warm grass, I had my first lessons in the beneficence of nature. I learned how the sun and the rain make to grow out of the ground every tree that is pleasant to the sight and good for food, how birds build their nests and live and thrive from land to land, how the squirrel, the deer, the lion and every other creature finds food and shelter. As my knowledge of things grew I felt more and more the delight of the world I was in. Long before I learned to

a . *Brassica capi =*   *tata purpurea et alba* ,
Geſtreiffter   Kopff-Kohl.
b. Brassica capitata   *cum flore,* Blühender Kopf-Kohl.
                                        c.

do a sum in arithmetic or describe the shape of the earth, Miss Sullivan had taught me to find beauty in the fragrant woods, in every blade of grass and in the curves and dimples of my baby sister's hand. She linked my earliest thoughts with nature, and made me feel that "birds and flowers and I were happy peers."

But about this time I had an experience which taught me that nature is not always kind. One day my teacher and I were returning from a long ramble. The morning had been fine, but it was growing warm and sultry when at last we turned our faces homeward. Two or three times we stopped to rest under a tree by the wayside. Our last halt was under a wild cherry tree a short distance from the house. The shade was grateful, and the tree was so easy to climb that with my teacher's assistance I was able to scramble to a seat in the branches. It was so cool up in the tree that Miss Sullivan proposed that we have our luncheon there. I promised to keep still while she went to the house to fetch it.

Suddenly a change passed over the tree. All the sun's warmth left the air. I knew the sky was black, because all the heat, which meant light to me, had died out of the atmosphere. A strange odour came up from the earth. I knew it, it was the odour that always precedes a thunderstorm, and nameless fear clutched at my heart. I felt absolutely alone, cut off from my friends and the firm earth. The immense, the unknown, enfolded me. I remained still and expectant; a chilling terror crept over me. I longed for my teacher's return; but above all things I wanted to get down from that tree.

There was a moment of sinister silence, then a multitudinous stirring of the leaves. A shiver ran through the tree, and the wind sent forth a blast that would have knocked me off had I not clung to the branch with might and main. The tree swayed and strained. The small twigs snapped and fell about me in showers. A wild impulse to jump seized me, but terror held me fast. I crouched down in the fork of the tree. The branches lashed about me. I felt the intermittent jarring that came now and then, as if something heavy had fallen and the shock had traveled up till it reached the limb I sat on. It worked my suspense up to the highest point, and just as I was thinking the tree and I should fall together, my teacher seized my hand and helped me down. I clung to her, trembling with joy to feel the earth under my feet once more. I had learned a new lesson—that nature "wages open war against her children, and under softest touch hides treacherous claws."

After this experience it was a long time before I climbed another tree.

The mere thought filled me with terror. It was the sweet allurement of the mimosa tree in full bloom that finally overcame my fears. One beautiful spring morning I was aware of a wonderful subtle fragrance in the air. I started up and instinctively stretched out my hands. It seemed as if the spirit of spring had passed through the summer-house. "What is it?" I asked, and the next minute I recognized the odour of the mimosa blossoms. I felt my way to the end of the garden, knowing that the mimosa tree was near the fence, at the turn of the path. Yes, there it was, all quivering in the warm sunshine, its blossom-laden branches almost touching the long grass. Was there ever anything so exquisitely beautiful in the world before? Its delicate blossoms shrank from the slightest earthly touch; it seemed as if a tree of paradise had been transplanted to earth. I made my way through a shower of petals to the great trunk and for one minute stood irresolute; then, putting my foot in the broad space between the forked branches, I pulled myself up into the tree. I had some difficulty in holding on, for the branches were very large and the bark hurt my hands. But I had a delicious sense that I was doing something unusual and wonderful, so I kept on climbing higher and higher, until I reached a little seat which somebody had built there so long ago that it had grown part of the tree itself. I sat there for a long, long time, feeling like a fairy on a rosy cloud. After that I spent many happy hours in my tree of paradise, thinking fair thoughts and dreaming bright dreams.

We read and studied out of doors, preferring the sunlit woods to the house. All my early lessons have in them the breath of the woods—the fine, resinous odour of pine needles, blended with the perfume of wild grapes. Seated in the gracious shade of a wild tulip tree, I learned to think that everything has a lesson and a suggestion. "The loveliness of things taught me all their use." Indeed, everything that could hum, or buzz, or sing, or bloom, had a part in my education—noisy-throated frogs, katydids and crickets held in my hand until, forgetting their embarrassment, they trilled their reedy note, little downy chickens and wildflowers, the dogwood blossoms, meadow-violets and budding fruit trees. I felt the bursting cotton-bolls and fingered their soft fiber and fuzzy seeds; I felt the low soughing of the wind through the cornstalks, the silky rustling of the long leaves, and the indignant snort of my pony, as we caught him in the pasture and put the bit in his mouth—ah me! How well I remember the spicy, clovery smell of his breath!

SOMETIMES I ROSE at dawn and stole into the garden while the heavy dew lay on the grass and flowers. Few know what joy it is to feel the roses pressing softly into the hand, or the beautiful motion of the lilies as they sway in the morning breeze. Sometimes I caught an insect in the flower I was plucking, and I felt the faint noise of a pair of wings rubbed together in a sudden terror, as the little creature became aware of a pressure from without.

Another favourite haunt of mine was the orchard, where the fruit ripened early in July. The large, downy peaches would reach themselves into my hand, and as the joyous breezes flew about the trees the apples tumbled at my feet. Oh, the delight with which I gathered up the fruit in my pinafore, pressed my face against the smooth cheeks of the apples, still warm from the sun, and skipped back to the house!

THE GEORGICS

 HAT MAKES the cornfields happy, under what constellation

It's best to turn the soil, my friend, and train the vine

On the elm; the care of cattle, the management of flocks,

The knowledge you need for keeping frugal bees:—all this

I'll now begin to relate. You brightest luminaries

Of the world, who head the year's parade across heaven's face:

Wine-god and kindly Harvest-goddess, if by your gift

Earth has exchanged the acorn for the rich ear of corn

And learnt to lace spring water with her discovered wine:

Scabiosa Sylvestris minor   Ornithogalum Arabicum.   *Genistella Tinctorum*
cærulea.

You Fauns, the tutelary spirits of country folk—

Dance here, you Fauns and Dryads—

Your bounties I celebrate. And you, Neptune, who first bade

The neighing horse start up from earth at your trident's stroke:

And you, the Forester, for whom three hundred head

Of milk-white cattle browse on the fruited bushes of Cea:

And you, leaving your native woods and the lawns of Arcadia,

Pan, master of flocks, if you love your Maenalus,

Come to my call and bless me: Minerva, who first discovered

The olive: the Boy who taught us the use of the crook-toothed plough:

Silvanus, bearing a young cypress plucked up by the roots:—

All gods and goddesses

Who care for the land, who nourish new fruits of the earth we sow not,

And send to our sown fields the plentiful rain from heaven.

You too, whatever place in the courts of the Immortals

Is soon to hold you—whether an overseer of cities

And warden of earth you'll be, Caesar, so that the great world

Honour you as promoter of harvest and puissant lord

Of the seasons, garlanding your brow with your mother's myrtle:

Or whether you come as god of the boundless sea, and sailors

Worship your power alone, and the ends of the earth pay tribute,

And Tethys gives all her waves to get you for son-in-law:

Or whether you make a new sign in the Zodiac, where amid the

Slow months a gap is revealed between Virgo and Scorpio

(Already the burning Scorpion retracts his claws to leave you

More than your share of heaven):—

Become what you may—and Hell hopes not for you as king,

And never may so ghastly a ruling ambition grip you,

Though Greece admire the Elysian Plains, and Proserpine

Care not to follow her mother who calls her back to earth—

Grant a fair passage, be gracious to this my bold design,

Pity with me the country people who know not the way,

Advance, and even now grow used to our invocations.

Pablo Neruda

ODE TO
THE ARTICHOKE

HE TENDER-

hearted artichoke

dressed in its armor,

built its modest cupola

and stood

erect,

impenetrable

beneath

The Superb Lily

London Published June 1799 by D. Thornton

DR. ROBERT JOHN THORNTON

{The Temple of Flora}

a lamina of leaves.

Around it,

maddened vegetables,

ruffling their leaves,

contrived

creepers, cattails,

bulbs and tubers to astound;

beneath the ground

slept

the red-whiskered carrot;

above, the grapevine

dried its runners,

bearers of the wine;

the cabbage

preened itself,

arranging its flounces;

oregano

perfumed the world,

while the gentle

artichoke

stood proudly in the garden,

clad in armor

burnished to a pomegranate

glow.

And then one day,

with all the other artichokes

in willow baskets,

our artichoke

set out to market

to realize its dream:

life as a soldier.

Amid ranks

never was it so martial

as in the fair,

white-shirted

men

among the greens

marshaled

the field

of artichokes,

close formations,

shouted commands,

and the detonation

of a falling crate.

But

look,

here comes

Maria

with her shopping basket.

Unintimidated,

she selects

our artichoke,

examines it, holds it to

the light as if it were an egg;

she buys it

she drops it

in a shopping bag

that holds a pair of shoes,

a cabbage head, and one

bottle

of vinegar.

Once home

and in the kitchen

she drowns it in a pot.

And thus ends

in peace

the saga

of the armored vegetable

we call the artichoke,

as

leaf by leaf

we unsheathe

its delights

and eat

the peaceable flesh

of its green heart.

The Vegetable Garden

HE WORK in the vegetables—Gertrude Stein was undertaking for the moment the care of the flowers and box hedges—was a full-time job and more. Later it became a joke, Gertrude Stein asking me what I saw when I closed my eyes, and I answered, Weeds. That, she said, was not the answer, and so weeds were changed to strawberries. The small strawberries, called by the French wood strawberries, are not wild but cultivated. It took me an hour to gather a small basket for Gertrude Stein's breakfast, and later when there was a

Brassica caulorapa prolifera, Kohlrüben mit Neben-Schoßl.

JOHANN WEINMANN

{Phytanthoza Iconographia}

Henderson pinx.   Burke & Lewis sculp.

The Sacred Egyptian Bean

London Published Dec.r 1 1804. by D.r Thornton.

plantation of them in the upper garden our young guests were told that if they cared to eat them they should do the picking themselves.

The first gathering of the garden in May of salads, radishes and herbs made me feel like a mother about her baby—how could anything so beautiful be mine. And this emotion of wonder filled me for each vegetable as it was gathered every year. There is nothing that is comparable to it, as satisfactory or as thrilling, as gathering the vegetables one has grown.

Later when vegetables were ready to be picked it never occurred to us to question what way to cook them. Naturally the simplest, just to steam or boil them and serve them with the excellent country butter or cream that we had from a farmer almost within calling distance. Later still, when we had guests and the vegetables had lost the aura of a new-born miracle, sauces added variety.

In the beginning it was the habit to pick all vegetables very young except beetroots, potatoes and large squash and pumpkins because of one's eagerness, and later because of their delicate flavour when cooked. That prevented serving sauces with some vegetables—green peas, string beans (indeed all peas and beans) and lettuces. There were exceptions, and for French guests this was one of them.

Ten Books of Architecture

O THESE DELICACIES we must add those of well-disposed Gardens and beautiful Trees, together with Porticoes in the Garden, where you may enjoy either Sun or Shade. To these add some little pleasant Meadow, with fine Springs of Water bursting out in different Places where least expected. Let the Walks be terminated by Trees that enjoy a perpetual Verdure, and particularly on that Side which is best sheltered from Winds, let them be enclosed with Box, which is presently injured and rotted by strong Winds, and especially by the least Spray from the Sea....

Chamæiris latifolia minima.

Chamæiris latifolia biflora.

Chamæiris latifolia
x Clusij.

Chamæiris latifolia
viii Clusii.

American Bog-Plants.

DR. ROBERT JOHN THORNTON

{The Temple of Flora}

Nor let there be wanting Cypress-trees cloathed with Ivy. Let the Ground also be here and there thrown into those Figures that are most commended in the Platforms of Houses, Circles, Semicircles, and the like, then surrounded with Laurels, Cedars, Junipers with their Branches intermixed, and twining one into the other....

The Ancients used to make their Walks into a Kind of Arbours by Means of Vines supported by Columns of Marble of the Corinthian Order, which were ten of their own Diameters in Height. The Trees ought to be planted in Rows exactly even, and answering to one another exactly upon straight Lines: and the Gardens should be enriched with rare Plants, and such are in most Esteem among the Physicians. It was a good agreeable Piece of Flattery among the ancient Gardeners, to trace their Masters Names in Box, or in sweet-smelling Herbs, in Parterres.... Nor am I displeased with the placing ridiculous Statues in Gardens, provided they have nothing in them obscene.

Victoria Sackville-West

The Legacy of Persia

 ONOUR THE GARDENER! that patient man

Who from his schooldays follows up his calling,

Starting so modestly, a little boy

Red-nosed, red-fingered, doing what he's told,

Not knowing what he does or why he does it,

Having no concept of the larger plan,

But gradually, (if the love be there,

Irrational as any passion, strong,)

Enlarging vision slowly turns the key

The Winged Passion Flower.

London, Published by D.r Thornton, June 1, 1802.

DR. ROBERT JOHN THORNTON

{The Temple of Flora}

a. *Abies Foemina*. Sapin Femelle. Fichte Weiblei.
b. *Abies Vulgaris*. Sapin Sauvage. Gemeine Tannen.
c. *Abies Picea mas*. Mast-baum.

JOHANN WEINMANN

{Phytanthoza Iconographia}

And swings the door wide open on the long

Vistas of true significance. No more

Is toil a vacant drudgery, when purport

Attends each small and conscientious task,

—As the stone-mason setting yard by yard

Each stone in place, exalting not his gaze

To measure growth of structure, or assess

That slow accomplishment, but in the end

Tops the last finial and, stepping back

To wipe the grit for the last time from eyes,

Sees that he built a temple,— so the true

Born gardener toils with love that is not toil

In detailed time of minutes, hours, and days,

Months, years, a life of doing each thing well;

The Life-line in his hand not rubbed away

As you might think, by constant scrape and rasp,

But deepened rather, as the line of Fate,

By earth imbedded in his wrinkled palm;

A golden ring worn thin upon his finger,

A signet ring, no ring of human marriage,

On that brown hand, dry as a crust of bread,

A ring that in its circle belts him close

To earthly seasons, and in its slow thinning

Wears out its life with his.

That hand, that broke with tenderness and strength

Clumps of the primrose and the primula,

Watched by a loving woman who desired

Such tenderness and strength to hold her close,

And take her passionate giving, as he held

His broken plants and set them in the ground,

New children; but he had no thought of her.

She only stood and watched his capable hand

Brown with the earth and golden with the ring,

And knew her part was small in his lone heart.

So comes he at the last to that long Paradise

Where grateful Pharaoh hews a mountain tomb

For the good gardener, the faithful slave,

(Slave not of royalty, but his own piety,)

Painting the vaulted roof of that deep cave

With fresco of imperishable fruit

Such as no earthly gardener ever grew,

Pale peaches and pale grapes, so healthy-heavy

Yet slung from tendrils of a filament

Too weak to bear a locust's weight. He sleeps,

No pest, no canker troubling that deep sleep

Under the pattern that he scarce divined.

THE DECAMERON

ANFILO HAD JUST reached the end of his story when the King, showing no compassion at all for Andreuola, looked at Emilia, giving her to understand that he wished her to follow those who had spoken; without any delay, she began:

Dear companions, the tale told by Panfilo leads me to tell you one which is unlike it in every respect except for the fact that just as Andreuola lost her lover in a garden, so too did the woman of whom I shall speak. She too was arrested, as was Andreuola, but she managed to free herself from the authorities not by force or virtue but rather by her unex-

Periclymenon perfoliatum.

Iuncus Cyperoidis palu, Clematis Daphnoides
dosus.   maior.

Periclymenon germanicum.

pected death. And as we have had occasion to remark in the past, no matter how willingly Love dwells in the homes of noblemen, he does not, because of this, scorn to rule in those of the poor; on the contrary, he sometimes demonstrates his powers in such places in order to make himself feared as the most powerful lord by the more wealthy. This will, if not completely at least in large part, become evident in my story, with which I shall have the pleasure of returning to our own city whence we have wandered so far during this day, speaking as we have about many different subjects in various parts of the world.

Not too long ago, then, there lived in Florence a girl named Simona, the daughter of a poor father, and she was quite beautiful and charming, considering her social condition, even though she was forced to go out and earn her bread with her own two hands, supporting herself by spinning wool. She was not, in spite of this, so poor in spirit that she did not long to receive love into her heart, which for some time now had been wanting to enter there through the pleasant words and deeds of a young man of no higher social status than herself, who worked for a wool merchant delivering wool to spin. Having thus received Love into her heart in the pleasing form

of this young man, whose name was Pasquino, and being filled with
passionate desires, but not daring to reveal them, she heaved a thousand
sighs, more burning than fire itself, with every yard of woolen thread she
wrapped around her spindle, recalling the one who had given her the
wool. Pasquino, for his part, became very concerned in seeing that his
master's wool was well spun, and acting as though the finished fabric were
to consist of only the wool Simona spun and that of no one else, he supervised
her more closely than the other girls. And so it happened that while one
was being attentive and the other was enjoying the attention, one of them
grew bolder than was his custom, while the other set aside her usual timidity
and modesty, and together they were united in mutual pleasure, which
was so enjoyable to both parties that rather than one waiting to be invited
by the other, it was, whenever they would meet, a case of who could be the
first to make the invitation.

And thus, as this pleasure of theirs continued from one day to the
next, growing always more passionate as it endured, it happened that
Pasquino told Simona that he would like very much for her to find some
way of getting to a certain garden where they could meet, and be together

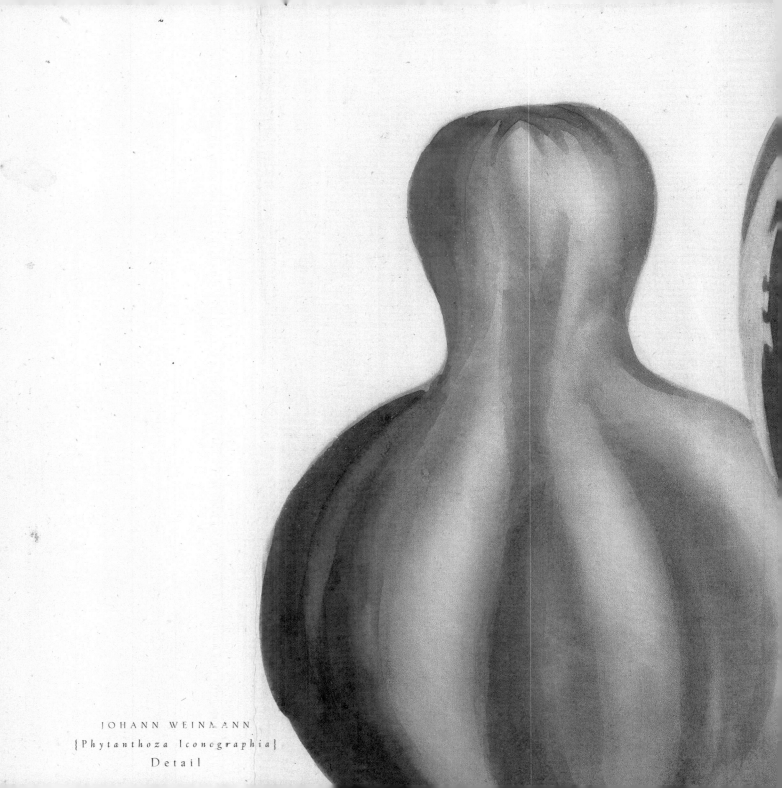

JOHANN WEINMANN
{Phytanthoza Iconographia}
Detail

more freely and arouse less suspicion. Simona replied that she would be happy to do so, and one Sunday, after lunch, having led her father to believe that she wanted to go to the Indulgences of San Gallo, she went with a companion of hers named Lagina to the garden Pasquino had told her about, and there she found him with a friend of his named Puccino but who was called "Stramba." Stramba and Lagina quickly fell for each other, so Pasquino and Simona went off to one part of the garden to pursue their own pleasures, leaving Stramba and Lagina to theirs in another.

There was in the part of the garden where Pasquino and Simona had gone a very large and beautiful sage bush at the foot of which they settled down to a long session of pleasure taking and talk of a picnic they were planning to have in that garden as soon as they were rested from their pleasure. Then Pasquino, turning toward the sage bush, plucked a leaf from it and began to rub his teeth and gums with it, declaring that sage was a good way of cleaning off everything that got stuck to your teeth and gums after eating. After rubbing them this way for a while, he returned to discussing the picnic they had just been talking about, but he had not said much before his whole face began to change, and following this change, in no time at all he lost his sight and his speech, and an instant later he was dead. When Simona saw this, she began to cry and scream, calling Stramba and Lagina; they quickly ran up to her, and when Stramba saw that Pasquino was not only dead but was already swollen and covered with dark blotches all over his face and body, he immediately cried:

"Ah, you wretched female, you've poisoned him!" He was making a great deal of noise and was heard by many of the people who lived near the garden; they ran toward the sound, and what with finding Pasquino dead and swollen and hearing Stramba on the one hand, lamenting and accusing Simona of having tricked Pasquino into taking poison, and Simona, on the other, not knowing how to explain things—for she was beside herself with grief from this unexpected misfortune that had taken away her lover—everyone there believed that things had happened just the way Stramba claimed they had.

And so she was arrested, and weeping all the while, she was taken off to the palace of the *podestà*. And once there, Stramba, Atticciato, and Malagevole (all friends of Pasquino who had arrived on the scene) made the accusations, at which point a judge was put on the case forthwith and

Cereus erectus altissim, Surinamensis.

JOHANN WEINMANN

{Phytanthoza Iconographia}

began to question her on the matter; but since he was unable to persuade himself that she had committed a criminal act or that she was guilty from the way she described the whole affair, he decided that he wanted to examine the dead body for himself and inspect the scene while in her presence, to see if it had happened the way she told it. Without any commotion, then, he had her brought to where Pasquino's body still lay, as swollen as a barrel, and then he went there himself, and gazing at the body in astonishment, he asked her how all this had come about. She went over to the sage bush, and having gone through every detail of the story once more, so that the judge might have all the facts concerning the misfortune which had occurred, she did just as Pasquino had done and rubbed one of those sage leaves against her teeth. While Stramba, Atticciato, and all of Pasquino's other friends and companions sneered in the judge's presence at her actions, shouting that it was all frivolous play-acting on her part and with even more insistence accusing her of being evil, declaring that nothing less than burning at the stake would be a fitting punishment for such evilness, the miserable girl, who was confused from her grief over her lost lover as well as from the fear of the punishment demanded by Stramba, went on rubbing her teeth with the sage, and then the same misfortune that happened to Pasquino, to the utter amazement of everyone who was present there, happened to her.

Oh, happy souls, whose fervent love and mortal lives both ended on the same day! And happier still, if you journeyed together to the same destination! And most happy of all, if Love exists in the next world, and you love each other as much as you did here on earth! But happiest of all is the soul of Simona, insofar as we who remain alive and have survived her are able to judge: for Fortune did not allow her innocence to fall before the accusations of Stramba, Atticciato, and Malagevole—who were nothing more than wool carders or even less—but instead, with a death similar to that of her lover, Fortune found for her a more appropriate way of freeing her from their infamous accusations and letting her follow the soul of her Pasquino, whom she loved so dearly.

The judge, as well as everyone else who was there, was so stunned by what had just occurred that he was at a loss for words and stood there for a long time; then, coming to his senses again, he said:

"It is clear that this sage bush is poisonous, which is quite unusual for a sage. And so that this bush may not harm anyone else in similar fashion, cut it down to the roots and set it on fire."

The man in charge of the garden did so in the judge's presence, and no sooner had he cut down the thick bush than the reason for the death of the two poor lovers became apparent. Under this sage bush was a toad of amazing size, whose venomous breath, they concluded, must have poisoned the sage bush. And since no one dared to go near this toad, they surrounded it with an enormous pile of firewood and burned it along with the sage bush; and thus ended the inquest of his lordship the judge into the death of poor Pasquino.

Pasquino, along with his Simona, swollen as they were, were buried by Stramba, Atticciato, Guccio the Mess, and Malagevole in the Church of San Paolo, of which they were, as chance would have it, parishioners.

Italo Calvino

THE SAND
GARDEN

 LITTLE COURTYARD COVERED with a white sand, thick-grained, almost gravel, raked in straight, parallel furrows or in concentric circles, around five irregular groups of stones or low boulders. This is one of the most famous monuments of Japanese civilization, the garden of rocks and sand of the Ryoanji of Kyoto, the image typical of that contemplation of the absolute to be achieved with the simplest means and without recourse to concepts capable of verbal expression, according to the teaching of the Zen monks, the most spiritual of Buddhist sects.

The rectangular enclosure of colorless sand is flanked on three sides by walls surmounted by tiles, beyond which is the green of trees. On the fourth side is a wooden platform, of steps, where the public can file by or linger and sit down. "Absorbed in this scene," explains the pamphlet offered to visitors, in Japanese and in English, signed by the abbot of the temple, "we, who think of ourselves as relative, are filled with serene wonder as we intuit Absolute Self, and our stained minds are purified."

Mr. Palomar is prepared to accept this advice on faith, and he sits on the steps, observes the rocks one by one, follows the undulations of the white sand, allows the undefinable harmony that links the elements of the picture gradually to pervade him.

Or, rather, he tries to imagine all these things as they would be felt by someone who could concentrate on looking at the Zen garden in solitude and silence. Because—we had forgotten to say—Mr. Palomar is crammed on the platform in the midst of hundreds of visitors, who jostle him on every side; camera lenses and movie cameras force their way past the elbows, knees, ears of the crowd, to frame the rocks and the sand from every angle, illuminated by natural light or by flashbulbs. Swarms of feet in wool socks step over him (shoes, as always in Japan, are left at the entrance); numerous offspring are thrust to the front row by pedagogical parents; clumps of uniformed students shove one another, eager only to conclude as quickly as possible this school outing to the famous monument; earnest visitors nodding their heads rhythmically check and make sure that everything written in the guidebook corresponds to reality and that everything seen in reality is also mentioned in the guide.

"We can view the garden as a group of mountainous islands in a great ocean, or as mountain tops rising above a sea of clouds. We can see it as a picture framed by the ancient mud walls, or we can forget the frame as we sense the truth of this sea stretching out boundlessly."

These "instructions for use" are contained in the leaflet, and to Mr. Palomar they seem perfectly plausible and immediately applicable, without effort, provided one is really sure of having a personality to shed, of looking at the world from inside an ego that can be dissolved, to become only a gaze. But it is precisely this outset that demands an effort of supplementary imagination, very difficult to muster when one's ego is glued into a solid crowd looking through its thousand eyes and walking on its thousand feet along the established itinerary of the tourist visit.

Must the conclusion be that the Zen mental techniques for

achieving extreme humility, detachment from all possessiveness and pride, require as their necessary background aristocratic privilege, and assume an individualism with so much space and so much time around it, the horizons of a solitude free of anguish?

But this conclusion, which leads to the familiar lament over a paradise lost in the spread of mass civilization, sounds too facile for Mr. Palomar. He prefers to take a more difficult path, to try to grasp what the Zen garden can give him, looking at it in the only situation in which it can be looked at today, craning his neck among other necks.

What does he see? He sees the human race in the era of great numbers, which extends in a crowd, leveled but still made up of distinct individualities like the sea of grains of sand that submerges the surface of the world.... He sees that the world, nevertheless, continues to turn the boulder-backs of its nature indifferent to the fate of mankind, its hard substance that cannot be reduced to human assimilation.... He sees the forms in which the assembled human sand tends to arrange itself along lines of movement, patterns that combine regularly and fluidity like the rectilinear or circular tracks of a rake.... And between mankind-sand and world-boulder there is a sense of possible harmony, as if between two nonhomogeneous harmonies: that of the nonhuman in a balance of forces

that seems not to correspond to any pattern, and that of human structures,

which aspires to the rationality of a geometrical or musical composition,

never definitive....

e.e. cummings

THE GARDEN

 HIS IS THE GARDEN: colours come and go,

frail azures fluttering from night's outer wing

strong silent greens serenely lingering,

absolute lights like baths of golden snow.

This is the garden: pursed lips do blow

upon cool flutes within wide glooms, and sing

(of harps celestial to the quivering string)

invisible faces hauntingly and slow.

Fritillaria iuncifolijs.

Tulipa viridis coloris.

Allium Vrsinum.

This is the garden. Time shall surely reap

and on Death's blade lie many a flower curled,

in other lands where other songs be sung;

yet stand They here enraptured, as among

the slow deep trees perpetual of sleep

some silver-fingered fountain steals the world.

PLATE LV

Black Antigua.

GEORGE BROOKSHAW

{A Collection of the Most Esteemed Fruits}

ACKNOWLEDGMENTS

Excerpt from *Alone* by Isaac Bashevis Singer ©1982 by Isaac Bashevis Singer. Reprinted by permission of Farrar, Straus, Giroux, Inc.

"The Ways of Wistaria" from *Flowers and Fruit* by Colette. Translation ©1986 by Farrar, Straus, Giroux, Inc. Reprinted by permission of Farrar, Straus, Giroux, Inc.

"Mushrooms" from *Collected Poems* by Sylvia Plath ©1960, 1965, 1971, 1981 by The Estate of Sylvia Plath. Reprinted by permission of HarperCollins Publishers.

"Hominy and Rain" from *Where Water Comes Together with Other Water* by Raymond Carver ©1984, 1985 by Raymond Carver. Reprinted by permission of Random House, Inc.

Excerpt from *The Georgics* by Virgil ©1947 by C. Day Lewis. Reprinted by permission of Oxford University Press, NY.

"Ode to the Artichoke" from *Selected Odes of Pablo Neruda* by Pablo Neruda, translated by Margaret Sayers Peden. ©1990 by the Regents of the University of California. Reprinted by permission of the University of California Press.

Excerpt from *The Alice B. Toklas Cook Book* by Alice B. Toklas. ©1954 by Alice B. Toklas. Copyright renewed ©1982 by Edward M. Burns. Reprinted by permission of HarperCollins Publishers.

"The Sand Garden" from *Mr. Palomar* by Italo Calvino, translated by William Weaver, ©1983 by Guilio Einaudi Editore, S.A., Torino. English translation ©1985 by Harcourt Brace Jovanovich, Inc. Reprinted by permission of Harcourt Brace Jovanovich, Inc.

"this is the garden" from *Collected Poems 1913-1962* by e.e. cummings. Published by MacGibbon & Kee, an imprint of HarperCollins Publisher Ltd. Reprinted by permission of HarperCollins Publishers and Liveright Publishing Corporation.

III.
Juncus Cyperoides palu,
stris.